Stewardship
ONE INCREDIBLE ADVENTURE!

George Haynes

STEWARDSHIP
ONE INCREDIBLE ADVENTURE!

Scripture quotations are from the Revised Standard Version of the Bible, copyright © 1946, 1952, and 1971 the Division of Christian Education of the National Council of the Churches of Christ in the United States of America. Used by permission. All rights reserved.

iUniverse books may be ordered through booksellers or by contacting:

iUniverse
1663 Liberty Drive
Bloomington, IN 47403
www.iuniverse.com
1-800-Authors (1-800-288-4677)

ISBN: 978-1-4917-9128-8 (sc)
ISBN: 978-1-4917-9129-5 (e)

Library of Congress Control Number: 2016903794

Print information available on the last page.

iUniverse rev. date: 06/15/2016

In this book, I have included Bible studies, personal reflections, provocative thoughts, and possible discussion starters that have to do with the concept and practice of stewardship.

Table of Contents

Introduction

It is my observation that a rather rigid tunnel vision of stewardship has put the whole concept, understanding, and practice in a mental straightjacket. Too many people believe stewardship is about money, *period*! It's like holding one piece of a jigsaw puzzle that has thousands more and exclaiming with great authority, "Here is the whole completed picture."

Stewardship is about so much more than money—a whole bunch more! We who are God's people need to wade right in and discover what stewardship really is.

The Bible studies, meditations, thought-provoking questions, and discussion starters I have included in this book are for one purpose— to expand your insight of, your grasp of, and your appreciation for the thrilling concept and incredible truth of stewardship. The whole purpose of this book is to broaden your vision and to deepen your understanding of stewardship.

I have one word of caution. Be prepared for change. You will find that this book is both stimulating and exciting. You may find yourself threatened by it. You may even be inclined to change some of your present patterns of living and giving or both.

Does this sound interesting? How about challenging? You bet it is! So let's get right to it.

Before and After

Before we go any further, let's take a moment or two to complete this sentence:

Stewardship is_____

_____

_____

_____

Good! Now, this one:

A steward is_____

_____

_____

_____

_____

Now forget this page and what you've written. We will come back to it later. When we do, write your new definitions below without looking at your previous answers. Then compare your answers from before with your new ones.

Stewardship is_____

_____

_____

_____

A steward is_____

_____

_____

_____

_____

Let's Begin with a Story from the Bible

For it will be as when a man going on a journey called his servants and entrusted to them his property; to one he gave five talents, to another two, to another one, to each according to his ability. Then he went away. He who had received the five talents went at once and traded with them; and he made five talents more. So also, he who had the two talents made two talents more. But he who had received the one talent went and dug in the ground and hid his master's money. Now after a long time the master of those servants came and settled accounts with them. And he who had received the five talents came forward, bringing five talents more, saying, "Master, you delivered to me five talents; here, I have made five talents more." His master said to him, "Well done, good and faithful servant; you have been faithful over a little, I will set you over much; enter into the joy of your master." And he also who had the two talents came forward, saying, "Master, you delivered to me two talents; here, I have made two talents more." His master said to him, "Well done, good and faithful servant; you have been faithful over a little, I will set you over much; enter into the joy of your master." He also who had received the one talent came forward, saying, "Master, I knew you to be a hard man, reaping where you did not sow, and gathering where you did not winnow; so I was afraid, and I went and hid your talent in the ground. Here you have what is yours." But his master answered him, "You wicked and slothful servant! You knew that I reap where I have not sowed, and gather where I have not winnowed? Then you ought to have invested my money with the bankers, and at my coming I should have received what was my own with interest. So take the talent from him, and give it to him who has the ten talents. For to everyone who has will more be given, and he will have abundance; but from him who has not, even what he has will be taken away. And cast the worthless servant into the outer darkness; there men will weep and gnash their teeth." (Matt. 25:14–30)

Please jot down the thoughts, ideas, or insights that came to you as you read this Bible story.

_____

_____

_____

_____

In a few words, answer the following questions. What happens in this story? What is Jesus trying to teach us through this story?

_____

_____

_____

_____

You might have noticed this is the second story Jesus tells in Matthew 25. Look at the first verse in this chapter. It says, "Then the kingdom of heaven shall be compared to." This is one terribly significant little phrase! It tells us, right off the bat, this is not just some cute little story Jesus is telling to entertain his listeners. This significant, little phrase tells us that this is the real-life story of the relationship which exists between the only true living God and you.

Read this story again and substitute the word *God* for *man* or *master* and your own name for the word *servant*. Wow! This really makes the story come to life, doesn't it? Okay, are you ready to move on?

Look once more Matthew 25:14. It tells us that the man, who was going on a journey, called his servants and "entrusted to them his property." If we substitute the word *God* for *man* or *master* and your own name for the word *servant*, as we did earlier, this powerful little package states that God entrusts his things to you and to me.

The word *entrusted* is powerful and is the key to getting to the very heart and soul of what stewardship is all about. It means to be entrusted with the responsibility of caring for, managing, using, and administering that which belongs to someone else. When we apply this to God, it means that you, I, and every other steward are trustees of God's property.

Let's review so that we will have a good firm grasp of this concept. A steward is a person who is entrusted by the rightful owner with the care, the management, the use, and the administration of the rightful owner's property or possessions. The management, care, use, and administration are the responsibility of the trustee or the one the owner has entrusted.

Keeping in mind that we are speaking here of the relationship that exists between you and God, it translates to something like this: God has chosen to entrust his property to you and me. God is still its rightful owner. God gives us the happy responsibility, dignity, and high honor of administering, caring for, using, and managing his property or, if you prefer, God's estate.

Let's look at another passage from the Bible that is very helpful.

> Then God said, "Let us make man in our image, after
> our likeness; and let them have dominion over the fish of
> the sea, and over the birds of the air, and over the cattle,

and over all the earth, and over every creeping thing that creeps upon the earth." So God created man in his own image, in the image of God he created him; male and female he created them. And God blessed them, and God said to them, "Be fruitful and multiply, and fill the earth and subdue it; and have dominion over the fish of the sea and over the birds of the air and over every living thing that moves upon the earth." (Gen. 1:26–28)

Zero in on just two words in this passage: *dominion* and *subdue*. These two words describe the responsibility and high privilege God gives to the human beings he has created. It says that they are to subdue the earth and to have dominion over the works of God's hands.

Drop everything and please take a few moments to do one thing. Think about the tremendous dignity, the sacred responsibility, and the happy privilege God gives you.

God honors and entrusts us with such a high and holy responsibility. Isn't it something that God has that kind of trust in us?

Hang on! Thoughts, ideas, and insights are probably tumbling in on you at such a fast pace you may not be able to put them in a nice, neat, or logical sequence. So let's wade through them together.

Before we go any further, I want you to read Matthew 25:14 one more time. "For it will be as when a man going on a journey called his servants and entrusted to them his property."

Why did I ask you to read this again? I want you to see that the man entrusted his *entire* estate and *all* his property. He put everything that belonged to him into his servants' hands. Now we are starting our ascent to some tremendous heights in learning.

When most folks think about stewardship, their thinking tends to be microscopic. They focus on just one thing—money. Other people include their time and talents. Sorry, but God will not permit his magnificent, magnanimous, monumental goodness, mercy, love, and grace to be squeezed into such teeny-weeny, miniscule dimensions. When God gives, he gives *everything*. When God entrusts, he entrusts *everything*.

Just to be certain we aren't thinking too small, let us pause and give God the opportunity to speak to us—both directly and through others.

Please read these verses again.

> Then God said, "Let us make man in our image, after
> our likeness; and let them have dominion over the fish of
> the sea, and over the birds of the air, and over the cattle,
> and over all the earth, and over every creeping thing that
> creeps upon the earth." So God created man in his own
> image, in the image of God he created them; male and
> female he created them. And God blessed them, and God
> said to them, "Be fruitful and multiply, and fill the earth
> and subdue it; and have dominion over the fish of the sea
> and over the birds of the air and over every living thing
> that moves upon the earth." (Gen. 1:26–28)

Please make a detailed list.

_____

_____

_____

_____

1. God instructs humans to subdue what?

_____

_____

_____

_____

2. God gives humans dominion over what?

_____

_____

_____

_____

We can sum it up by saying that God entrusted human beings with subduing and having dominion over everything he made. To reinforce this idea, listen to the strong amen and exclamation point of Psalm 24:1, "The earth is the LORD's and the fulness thereof, the world and those who dwell therein."

Also listen to King David's moving prayer found in 1 Chronicles 29 as he prays a dedication over the offerings and gifts he and the Israelites have given to build a temple to the Lord.

Thine, O LORD, is the greatness, and the power, and the glory, and the victory, and the majesty; *for all that is in the heavens and the earth is thine.* (verse 11, emphasis added)

But who am I, and what is my people, that we should be able thus to offer willingly? *For all things come from thee, and of thy own have we given thee.* (verse 14, emphasis added)

Let's rehearse it just one more time:

- The earth and everything in it is the Lord's.
- The whole creation is the work of God.
- God is the maker, the owner, and the Lord of all creation.
- God has entrusted all creation to your hands and to mine to be cared for, used, managed, and administered.
- Everything we have and everything we are comes from God.

Wait. We have forgotten something—a terribly important something! Well, we didn't forget it but are just getting to it. Turn one more time to Matthew 25. This time as you read, listen to what the servant says in verses

24 and 25, and listen to what the man repeats and reinforces in verses 26 and 27.

First, let's read about the servant. "Master, I knew you to be a hard man, reaping where you did not sow, and gathering where you did not winnow; so I was afraid, and I went and hid your talent in the ground. Here, you have what is yours" (verses 24–25).

Now, let's read the master's response. "You wicked and slothful servant! You knew that I reap where I have not sowed, and gather where I have not winnowed? Then you ought to have invested my money with the bankers, and at my coming I should have received what was my own with interest" (verses 26–27).

Because the servants were entrusted with property, possessions, and everything that belonged to their master, they couldn't just do whatever they darn well pleased with it. They had to manage what was entrusted to them according to their master's interests, concerns, desires, and will.

What I am trying to help you understand is that because we are servants entrusted with God's possessions, we have some things to consider before we decide how we will care for, use, or manage them. We must ask ourselves the following questions:

1. How does my Master want me to use his things?
2. How would my Master care for and manage these things?
3. What is my Master's will?
4. What is his vision for all this?
5. What are his hopes and desires for his estate?

Once we know the answers to these questions, we can discharge our stewardship responsibly. We will live in the midst of, handle, manage, administer, and care for God's creation the way he wants us to. Responsibility and accountability are two important words that are vital ingredients of stewardship.

Let's take time again to simply reflect upon the glorious truth that we are in partnership with God to care, to manage, to use, and to minister his entire physical creation. Imagine that.

The Other Side of Stewardship

We're going to move into a different gear now. Let's turn the stewardship coin over and look at its other side. Stewardship has another completely different dimension. When this story states that God entrusts his whole estate into our hands, we are not only talking about physical things but also about spiritual things. Please understand that stewardship involves every bit as much of the spiritual as it does the physical and personal.

The everything God has entrusted to us for care, use, administration, and management includes God's will, plans, desires, hopes, and vision in the area of redeeming, reconciling, and saving.

Now, don't just take my word for it. God's spokesman, the apostle Paul, says,

> If any one is in Christ, he is a new creation; the old has passed away, behold, the new has come. All this is from God, who through Christ reconciled us to himself and *gave us the ministry of reconciliation*; that is, in Christ God was reconciling the world to himself, not counting their trespasses against them, and *entrusting to us the message of reconciliation*. So we are ambassadors for Christ, God making his appeal through us. (2 Cor. 5:17–20, emphasis added)

Look at verses 18 and 19. Two important concepts are *given to us* and *entrusted to us*. What are these two things? They are "the ministry of reconciliation" and the "the message of reconciliation." That's awesome! We're talking about the forgiveness of sins. We're talking about reconciling people to God and to one another. We're talking about demonstrating the good news of God's love in Jesus Christ. This is in the realm of holy baptism, the Eucharist, the church, and prayer. We're dealing with such matters as evangelism, inclusiveness, and world missions.

All this is stewardship. It also is a magnificent trust from God. For this too, God has seen fit to choose us in Christ, to call us by name, and to lay this cloak of responsibility upon us. If we thought we had a truly glorious partnership with God before this, look at it and consider it now.

Stewardship embraces all aspects, phases, and dimensions of our lives—physical, social, emotional, spiritual, public, and private. The stewardship God has entrusted to you and me involves absolutely everything—the whole of God's physical creation, which includes the earth, people, things, and the whole of God's great redemptive purpose and plan.

I am every bit as much duty bound in this realm we call spiritual. My first responsibility here, too, is to discover what my Master's will is. What are my Master's hopes, vision, and plan in this facet of my life?

Now you can see the vital role the church, the Word, the sacraments, the fellowship of believers, and prayer have in making those kinds of determinations. More than that, you can see how vital each of these is in equipping, enabling, and empowering us to live out what we are expected and required to do in this realm, if we are to be good and faithful servants.

You know, the longer we contemplate these things, the more glorious, magnificent, and astounding they become. The more we see these things become glorious, awesome, exhilarating, and meaningful, the more we will see and appreciate what it means to be called children of God and his stewards.

I don't know about you, but I'm ready to dig deeper to find more practical applications of these truths we have been talking about. I have a feeling that such excavations could be both stimulating and challenging. Please join me.

Chapter 1

Stewardship of Self

I am somebody, 'cause God don't make no junk.

In this chapter, we will begin where our conversation about the physical creation left off in the last chapter. Let's begin with the physical creation we are most familiar with—ourselves. Let's talk about the stewardship of life and self. Two places we'll want to go for resource information are (1) the Bible and (2) Luther's Catechism.

Let's begin with the Bible.

> Then God said, "Let us make man in our image, after our likeness" … So God created man in his own image, in the image of God he created him; male and female he created them. (Gen. 1:26–27)

> Then the LORD God formed man of dust from the ground, and breathed into his nostrils the breath of life; and man became a living being. (Gen. 2:7)

The self and the life are the creations of and a gift from God the Father, the Creator.

You may already know it by heart, but just in case you don't or it has become a bit rusty, here are the words for you:

> I believe that God has created me and all that exists; that he has given and still preserves my body and soul with all

their powers. He provides me with food and clothing, home and family, daily work, and all that I need from day to day. God also protects me in time of danger and guards me from every evil.

It goes on to state, "all this God does out of fatherly and divine goodness and mercy, though I do not deserve it."

You may want to spend a few moments just pondering this wonderful truth. The very fact that I am and even have life and being is a gift from God. All that I am and all that I have is a sheer unadulterated gift from God.

Before you do anything else, mark this page and take this book outside with you. Do it now. Let's experience how marvelous a creation we actually are. Ready?

Here are some activities you might want to try while you are outside:

1. Take three good deep breaths and then exhale them.
2. Feel your heart beating or take your pulse.
3. Listen. What do you hear? A bird, an automobile, voices, the wind in the trees, an airplane, a dog barking? Keep listening.
4. Look at the various colors, sizes, shapes, and shades around you.
5. Touch grass, wood, cement, cloth, and metal.
6. Smell a flower, the air, and perfume or aftershave.

Part of your standard equipment is your senses' ability to perceive, your thinking processes, and your ability to respond. These are all gifts from God. God has made you and all the equipment you need. You are absolutely one magnificent, marvelous being.

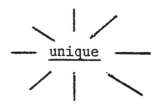

There is no other person exactly like you anywhere in the entire universe. You are God's own, deliberate, purposeful creation.

Let's slowly savor each delicious thought about how fully, intimately, and personally we are known and loved by our Creator and heavenly Father as we read Psalm 139:1–18.

> O LORD, thou hast searched me and known me! Thou knowest when I sit down and when I rise up; thou discernest my thoughts from afar. Thou searchest out my path and my lying down, and art acquainted with all my ways. Even before a word is on my tongue, lo, O LORD, thou knowest it altogether. Thou dost beset me behind and before, and layest thy hand upon me. Such knowledge is too wonderful for me; it is high, I cannot attain it. Whither shall I go from thy Spirit? Or whither shall I flee from thy presence? If I ascend to heaven, thou art there! If I make my bed in Sheol, thou art there! If I take the wings of the morning and dwell in the uttermost parts of the sea, even there thy right hand shall lead me, and thy right hand shall hold me. If I say, "Let only darkness cover me, and the light about me be night," even the darkness is not dark to thee, the night is bright as the day; for darkness is as light with thee. For thou didst form my inward parts, thou didst knit me together in my mother's womb. I praise thee, for thou art fearful and wonderful. Wonderful are thy works! Thou knowest me right well; my frame was not hidden from thee, when I was being made in secret, intricately wrought in the depths of the earth. Thy eyes beheld my unformed substance; in thy book were written, every one of them, the days that were formed for me, when as yet there was none of them. How precious to me are thy thoughts,

> O God! How vast is the sum of them! If I could count them, they are more than the sand. When I awake, I am still with thee.

Isn't this great? More is on the way.

Right now, rejoice, give thanks, and realize that you are whole and complete and that your life is part of that *everything* God has entrusted to you.

We have one last item. Write your age in the blanks:

A. _____years
B. _____months
C. _____days

Now let's convert everything into days. Multiply A by 365.25 and write the total down in the A blank. Convert B to days and write it down in the B blank. Write C down again in the C blank. Then add all three and put your total in the total days blank.

A. _____days
B. _____days
C. _____days

Total: _____days

On many separate and individual occasions, your heavenly Father made the conscious decision to grant you the gift of another day of life. Think of it and marvel over it.

Let's say it again, "I am a gift from God. My life and I are part of the trust God has placed in my hands." Doesn't this phrase tell us we should be good stewards of ourselves and our lives? Doesn't it point out the importance of taking care of ourselves? Do you take care of yourself? What kind of food do you eat? How much food do you eat? Do you exercise? Do you recreate or "wreckreate"? Do you take time off from work? Do you allow yourself to relax?

Make a covenant with yourself to take a brisk walk outside. While walking, listen, look, sense, and greet others. Make a covenant with yourself to eat only one helping of good, nutritious, wholesome food and to drink eight glasses of water each day. Make a covenant with yourself to take one day each week as a Sabbath where you will find physical, mental, and spiritual refreshment and renewal. Make a covenant with yourself to think that you are here on earth because that is God's wonderful plan, that your work is your calling, and that each day and its activities are portions of your pilgrimage. You owe it to yourself and to God to make such covenants.

While you're thinking about all this, remember, every other person is also a creation of God. Each person should be received, cherished, respected, and accepted with thanksgiving like every other gift and blessing God so graciously gives us. Every other person is a gift from God to you just as you are a gift to that person. This gift is special and fragile. So please handle it with care.

Celebrate your personhood. Celebrate your uniqueness. Celebrate *you*. Do you see how much fun stewardship can be?

Shall we talk a little bit more about this idea of the stewardship of self? In particular, I want us to consider our spiritual self.

Let's talk, for the next few moments, about your devotional life, which means prayer, meditation, Bible study, reflection, worship, and fellowship with others. How's your devotional life? Are you growing spiritually? Have you read any good devotional books lately? How's your prayer life?

Let's make no bones about it. Not one of us has the native resources, strength, wit, and wisdom to make it by ourselves. We face pressures, decisions, influences, temptations, and fears, both within without, that are more than we can handle.

Even more to the point, we are created for fellowship with God, and without that fellowship, we are not complete. We aren't all there, so to speak.

The psalmist cries, "My soul thirsts for God, for the living God" (Ps. 42:2). Do you feel that way too sometimes?

It's like Psalm 63:1 says, "O God, thou art my God, I seek thee, my soul thirsts for thee; my flesh faints for thee, as in a dry and weary land where no water is." Yes, you've experienced that too. Good. Because it makes you keenly aware of the urgent need you have for fellowship with God through his Word, prayer, and meditation. This is where God speaks with you and you speak with God.

Sometimes it's even higher and deeper than that, isn't it? It's more than an urgent need. It is the desire to be with the One you love, and you can hardly wait for those moments, times, and opportunities. At its heart, the Christian faith is just one great big love affair with God, isn't it?

If we're talking about pleasure, we're talking about fellowship with God. If we're talking about richness, we're talking about fellowship with God. If we're talking about satisfaction, we're talking about fellowship with God. If we're talking about stimulating, challenging, and a sense of calling, we're talking about fellowship with God. Fellowship with God is devotions, worship, sacrament, and prayer. It is *koinonia* with God's people.

I want you to approach stewardship of self from another angle by participating in the following activities.

(1) Do something radical and daring.

Get four or five other people to join you. Swear everyone to absolute secrecy. This is the plan: All participants must save their garbage for ten days. Plan it so that the tenth day falls on a Saturday. On Saturday night, take all the garbage and scatter it everywhere inside your church building. Spread the mess down the center aisle, the side aisles, all over the pews, chancel area, and altar—everywhere!

You refuse to do it, don't you? This entire idea utterly repulses you, doesn't it? Do that to the church? Never! You would never be guilty of defiling and desecrating the temple of the Lord in this way.

Good for you! However, keep this activity in the back of your mind, please. The whole point of this will become clear shortly. Do this next activity instead.

(2) Take a brief journey through your city.

You may either go out and actually make this brief journey or you can sit right where you are and let this be a mental journey. As you make your journey, look at or think about the various church buildings and synagogues in your city. Really look at them or picture them in your mind's eye.

You probably see different shapes and various sizes, right? Some are old, some are new, and some are in between, right? Do you see a variety of color schemes and different exteriors? Some are brick, some are wood, some are steel, and some are stone.

In spite of all these differences, what is it they all have in common? Even though there may be different shapes, sizes, ages, colors, backgrounds, and locations in the community, every one of them is a temple of the Lord.

You may wonder where I am going with this. I'm taking you to 1 Corinthians 3:16–17, which says, "Do you not know that you are God's temple and that God's Spirit dwells in you? ... For God's temple is holy, and that temple you are." Read that again, please. You are the temple in which God's Spirit dwells.

This house of God, like every other one in your community, deserves the very best of care just because it *is* the house of God.

Because you are God's temple and the dwelling place of his Spirit, you will want to do everything you possibly can to make it as strong, beautiful, comfortable, attractive, and clean as you possibly can.

Let me further explain. First of all, let's focus on the thought that you are the Holy Spirit's temple. To me, this says something very definite about the types of books we should be reading, television shows we should be watching, movies or types of entertainment we should be attending, and jokes, stories, and remarks we should be listening to.

Are you following me? Let's go straight to Jesus's own words. He says, "The eye is the lamp of the body. So, if your eye is sound, your whole body will be full of light; but if your eye is not sound, your whole body will be full of darkness" (Matt. 6:22–23). He also says, "You brood of vipers! how can you speak good, when you are evil? For out of the abundance of the heart the mouth speaks" (Matt. 12:34).

I feel these verses are telling us that if we continually accept and receive immorality, violence, dirty jokes, lewd pictures, and so on through our eyes and ears, and if these are like coins we steadily deposit into our memory banks, when the time comes to make withdrawals, we cannot bring forth anything other than what we have deposited, right? If we continually bring filth and garbage into this temple of the Lord, this temple is going to be so filthy and cluttered the Holy Spirit is not only going to be uncomfortable but also will not be able to find a place there to dwell.

Furthermore, we so pollute our bodies with drugs, alcohol, and tobacco that we effectively suffocate and squeeze the very life out of the Spirit, whose temple we are supposed to be. Isn't it possible that physical abuse, stress, and fatigue make a poor and ineffective environment for the Spirit of God? All these things interrupt the Spirit's resident status.

I am not preaching at you but am trying to provoke some serious thoughts and decisions on your part regarding you being God's temple and the dwelling place of God's Holy Spirit. We simply cannot divorce that truth from the implications it has on our physical, spiritual, ethical, and behavioral health. This is so important I feel it should have a proper place as part of our table talk, don't you?

Chapter 2

Stewardship of Earth, Water, and Air

+ with a request that this book be printed on recycled paper

I am impressed and absolutely awed by the magnificently thorough and thoroughly magnificent way in which God created the world. God prepared creation for the arrival of human beings on the earth. He made these humans to inhabit the world, to subdue the earth, and to have dominion over all his marvelous and magnificent handiwork.

You probably know it by heart, but please read and experience that profound account of the creation, one more time, as it is recorded in Genesis 1:1–2:3. Please get your Bible and read those verses now. After reading them, sit quietly for a moment. Let the glory, majesty, and wonder of God and his creation enfold you. It is utterly awesome. Psalm 8:1 tells us, "O Lord, our Lord, how majestic is thy name in all the earth!"

"It's a great, wide, wonderful world we live in." Whoever wrote those words really knew what he was talking about, didn't he? Everything we humans need for our lives and well-being is here. God has given us every ingredient we need to make our physical existences on earth satisfying and productive. Our good and gracious heavenly Father has packed every nook and cranny with additional blessings for our benefit. So fully has God blessed this creation of his that every day we are still uncovering processes or materials we never dreamed were there. In God's merciful goodness, He allows us to stumble onto one or leads us to another through the "You're getting warmer, warmer …" game called research.

What is so absolutely thrilling and, at the same time, sobering is this. God stepped back, surveyed the entire physical universe, including the human realm created in the very image of God, and rendered the divine judgement that it was very good. And then, my dear friends, the Creator, owner, and Lord of the entire physical creation crowned us with additional glory, honor, and dignity by putting that physical creation squarely into our hands as a sacred trust!

The living and only true God entrusted and charged us with the regal responsibility of managing and caring for that creation. We are God's chosen, appointed, and trusted stewards. The Lord's word to the humans he had created was, "I'm putting you in charge." This is awesome, awesome, awesome.

Since we're discussing the stewardship of the earth, I can think of no better place to begin than with the physical description of the Promised Land into which God was bringing the Israelites. Let's read Deuteronomy 8:7–9.

> For the Lord your God is bringing you into a good land, a land of brooks of water, of fountains and springs, flowing forth in valleys and hills, a land of wheat and barley, of vines and fig trees and pomegranates, a land of olive trees and honey, a land in which you will eat bread without scarcity, in which you will lack nothing, a land whose stones are iron, and out of whose hills you can dig copper.

Did something click as you read those verses? Did you find yourself thinking, *That's a pretty accurate description of the place I'm living in now.* You might have to make some slight adjustments to your geography and geology. You might have to substitute the word *apple* for *pomegranate*. However, you are still blessed.

Let's take a physical inventory of your area. Please list the following items:

- Two kinds of trees
- Two fruits
- Two vegetables

- Two grain crops
- At least one natural resource
- A nearby body of water

We are doing this exercise to remind ourselves of the good land into which the Lord our God has brought us and has given into our hands as a trust for stewarding. Let's remember that these good resources and the overwhelming abundance are all a gift from God. God placed all of it here as he created and blessed the land. All these things are important and vital parts of the physical creation God has entrusted to us when he appointed us to subdue and to have dominion over the earth.

Please understand that *subdue* and have *dominion over* do not mean

1. to rape;
2. to pillage,
3. to waste;
4. to squander;
5. to deface; or
6. to destroy.

They do mean

1. to conserve;
2. to plan;
3. to share;
4. to nurture;
5. to improve;
6. to respect;
7. to protect; and
8. to be thankful for.

Now we are moving into the territory of subduing and dominion as they relate to stewardship. It is the careful management and administration of the land, its resources, and its potential in accordance with God's will. This is what brings the Christian steward into direct and personal involvement with such issues as pollution, toxic waste, land use, conservation, hunger, justice, zoning, pesticides, the ozone layer, reforestation, landfill, restoration of topography, miles per gallon, and consumption of goods and resources.

Rather than simply talk about this, let's actually do some hands-on learning. How do we do this? We can take one specific resource—in this case water—and conduct the following two simple tests.

Brushing Your Teeth, Part 1

For this test, you will need a large container that will hold water and has liquid amounts printed on the side of it. Put the container in your sink. Turn the water on and let it run while you wet your brush; put toothpaste on your brush; brush your teeth; rinse your mouth; and rinse your brush.

Now check your container and write down the amount of water you used:

Amount of water you used_____

Brushing Your Teeth, Part 2

For this test, you will need a six-ounce cup. Fill the cup with water. Follow the same steps listed for Part 1 but only use water from the cup.

Now we can compare the amount of water used in each test.

Amount of water used in Part 1 _____

Amount of water used in Part 2_____

Which test represents the best stewardship of water? Part 2 does.

One observation I have made regarding water is that when we shower we use only one-third the amount of water that we use when we take a bath. Do you see what a difference we can make when we are aware and translate that awareness into practice?

As we discuss the conservation of natural resources, we can be thankful that in recent years the car's miles per gallon has shown a dramatic increase. It is not unusual to see cars advertised as being capable of thirty-five, forty, or more miles per gallon on the highway. We still need to recognize, however, that as we exceed sixty-five miles per hour, our miles per gallon decrease 1 percent for each mile we go faster. When it is safe to do so, I reduce my car's speed to fifty-five miles per hour and watch my miles per gallon jump to forty-three.

Why are we all in such a great big hurry anyway? We're zipping here and there so fast, we hardly get an opportunity to enjoy the beautiful creation around us. When was the last time you simply drove down to the waterfront, turned off your car's ignition, and watched the seabirds or listened to the surf lapping gently against the shore?

When you were a child, do you remember lying on the grass and watching the clouds overhead? You turned on your imagination and saw all kinds of neat things—a cloud shaped like a dog or a human face. When was the last time you walked barefoot through the grass, waded in the water, or bent down and smelled a flower? Have you ever taken a blade of grass, tucked it between your thumbs, and blown on it to make music? Today, you might want to try some of these things again. It could prove to be downright delightful!

Are you aware it takes a full six ounces of petroleum product, which is a nonrenewable resource, to make one aluminum can? Once we use up that petroleum, we will have no way to obtain more.

Recycling really makes a great deal of sense, doesn't it? It not only conserves natural resources but also puts a little extra money in our pockets.

Here is a way you can conserve natural resources and have additional money for starting new ministries. Put some sacks or boxes in your pantry. Deposit aluminum cans in one, glass in another, and paper in the third. When your containers are full, go sell it for cash. Put the money in an envelope and mark it "For New Ministries." Put the envelope in the offering plate on Sunday morning.

Let's talk about fertilizers for a moment. We point an accusing finger at the farmer for all those pesticides and fertilizers he uses. We know that all this runs into streams, rivers, and lakes. In point of fact, the fertilizers, pesticides, and chemicals that city dwellers use to make their lawns green and lush, flowers strong and pretty, and insects and bugs sorry they showed up create greater pollution than what comes from the farm.

We need to stop pointing the finger. There is guilt on both sides. We all must become far more serious about the uses and abuses of fertilizers and pesticides. How about using natural fertilizers? Can animals, fowl, and fish assist us in preserving our natural resources as we produce needed fertilizers? If we use organic fertilizers, we can conserve chemicals, reduce pollution, save money, and protect the ozone layer by not using the compressed stuff.

Where can you get these natural fertilizers? If you have a friend who is a farmer or a rancher, ask him if he will give you some. If you don't, try to get a farmer or rancher to sell you some. It's one idea to get you thinking about what you can do to be a good steward of the land.

Another idea would be to plant a tree, even if today is not Arbor Day! Reforestation is a wonderful process. Trees produce, capture, and conserve such elements as oxygen and nitrogen. They affect the amount and frequency of rainfall and temperature. So today or sometime this week plant a tree. You might even want to buy a live Christmas tree this year and then plant it after Christmas.

Here are a few other practical thoughts I'd like to share with you. Why is it that before building housing developments, shopping centers, or factories, we don't first take soil samples and put those types of structures where the soil tests least promising for agricultural or floral products? Instead, we arbitrarily place those buildings on rich and productive soil. We should use our influence to decide where houses, factories, and waste disposal facilities are to be built. That way, human and industrial wastes won't add to our already overtaxed equipment and facilities. Wouldn't it be great if the government required a certain amount of acreage to be set aside for parks as part of the plan for each housing development? Stewards of creation concern themselves with restoring and preserving streams, lakes, and waterways so they won't become conveyer belts and depositories for trash and refuse but remain clean and fresh so fish and bathers may swim in them.

No wonder all creation groans and waits for the day of its deliverance and redemption. It is so choked in waste, blinded by smog, scarred by strip-mining, and tattooed by housing developments, God must have difficulty recognizing his handiwork.

Let's examine a statement made by the apostle Paul in 2 Corinthians 9:8. He says, "And God is able to provide you with every blessing in abundance, so that you may always have enough of everything and may provide in abundance for every good work." This is terrific. There's an exciting stewardship principle spelled out for us here. Not only does God provide in such measure that our prayer, "Give us this day our daily bread," is met in full and truly answered but also goes beyond this. He blesses us so abundantly that we have enough to share with other people. We can actually be the means through which our neighbor's prayer for daily bread can be answered as well. Not only does God permit each one of us to experience his love and goodness in our own lives but also allows us to be the means by which someone else experiences God's love and goodness. Fantastic! This is one more way in which God permits us to work hand in hand with him so that his good and gracious will, desires, and purposes may be realized.

See how exciting, meaningful, and satisfying this life of stewardship can be? Isn't God absolutely great for giving us this stewardship? Amen!

Chapter 3

When Stewardship Marries Evangelism

The Father, Son, and Holy Spirit Requests
the Honor of Your Presence

For some people, it may be the first time they have ever attended the wedding of stewardship and evangelism, but the Holy Scripture frequently celebrates that marriage, doesn't he?

To help us understand this process, let's read 2 Corinthians 5:17–20:

> Therefore, if any one is in Christ, he is a new creation; the old has passed away, behold, the new has come. All this is from God, who through Christ reconciled us to himself and gave us the ministry of reconciliation; that is, in Christ God was reconciling the world to himself, not counting their trespasses against them, and entrusting to us the message of reconciliation. So we are ambassadors for Christ, God making his appeal through us.

To understand how the knot is tied between stewardship and evangelism, take another look at verses 18 and 19. "All this is from God, who through Christ reconciled us to himself and gave us the ministry of reconciliation; that is, in Christ God was reconciling the world to himself, not counting their trespasses against them, and entrusting to us the message of reconciliation."

Notice the word *gave* in verse 18 and *entrusted* in verse 19. That's stewardship talk.

In verse 18, what is given? _____

In verse 19, what is entrusted? _____

Answers: the ministry of reconciliation (verse 18) and the message of reconciliation (verse 19). They are both given to us as stewards of the Lord.

We have entered into that area of our partnership with God where we are coworkers with God and with one another. Together we carry out the mission of proclaiming the gospel and being witnesses. We are to share and demonstrate God's love in Christ—the love that makes it possible for people to receive and experience forgiveness of sins, a restored relationship with God, victory over death and the grave, a whole new lease on life, and the joy of triumphant living in and with the Lord.

Have you noticed in Holy Scripture as well as in your own experience, the beautiful process that occurs as Christ's saving love works in a person's life? As quickly as the Holy Spirit brings a person to faith in Jesus Christ, he calls that person out of the world and gathers him or her into the church and the company of other believers.

In that community, the Spirit nurtures faith, bestows spiritual gifts, equips and empowers believers for their callings, and then sends them right back into the world to be God's agents for change and ministers of reconciliation.

Hold it! What happens between the Spirit gathering the believer into the community of faith and that person being empowered and sent out as an agent of change? What takes place during that time? What are the means the Holy Spirit uses in the congregation to do his work to nurture, enlighten, equip, and empower? The answer is ministries.

The Holy Spirit uses the ministries of your congregation to nurture people's faith, to provide insights into the Word of God, to equip and empower believers for witness and service, and to disciple them in their daily work, play, and living.

Who provides these ministries in your congregation? How are these ministries maintained in your congregation? The answer involves you. As you, child of God, and others like you offer, with joy and thanksgiving, yourselves, your time, and your possessions, these ministries take place. This whole business, from start to finish, is stewardship, and yet, at the same time, it is evangelism.

So as a follower of Christ, it is my happy responsibility to commit my God-given abilities, time, and possessions to Christ's church, first to the congregation of which I am a member, then to the synod, and finally to the whole church. The gifts of self, time, and possessions make ministries happen. Those ministries make it possible for mission to be realized!

First, let me define the word *church* here. It is the communion of saints, the community of believers in Christ, and the faith community. Now understand that God has entrusted the gospel to you, to me, and to other believers. God has entrusted us with the good news, which is, as Saint Paul reminds us, "the power of God for salvation" (Rom. 1:16).

Saint Paul further points out to us, "Because, if you confess with your lips that Jesus is Lord and believe in your heart that God raised him from the dead, you will be saved … For, 'everyone who calls upon the name of the Lord will be saved'" (Rom. 10:9, 13). In another passage he says, "But how are men to call upon him in whom they have not believed? And how are they to believe in him of whom they have never heard? And how are they to hear without a preacher [witness]? And how can men preach [witness)] unless they are sent? … So faith comes from what is heard, and what is heard comes by the preaching of Christ" (Rom. 10:14–15, 17).

Saint Paul is pointing out that the Spirit works through the proclamation of the good news to create the miracle of faith that makes a person become a believer. To whom has the Lord entrusted that good news message? Here are some verses that tell us:

> And Jesus came and said to them, "All authority in heaven and on earth has been given to me. Go therefore and make disciples of all nations, baptizing them in the name of the Father and of the Son and of the Holy Spirit, teaching them to observe all that I have commanded you; and, lo, I am with you always, to the close of the age." (Matt. 28:18–20)

Peace be with you. As the Father has sent me, even so I send you. (John 20:21)

But you are a chosen race, a royal priesthood, a holy nation, God's own people, *that* you may declare the wonderful deeds of him who called you out of darkness into his marvelous light. (1 Peter 2:9, emphasis added)

But you shall receive power when the Holy Spirit has come upon you; and you shall be my witnesses in Jerusalem and in all Judaea and Samaria and to the end of the earth. (Acts 1:8)

Who does the Lord entrust the good news message to? Who is the Lord counting on to publish that gospel? He is counting on his disciples. Who are his disciples? They are church, the believers, and (write your name here) _____.

The Lord ties a firm knot between stewardship and evangelism in this wedding, doesn't he? When we talk about the gospel, we need to take the next logical step to the sacraments, right? The sacraments represent the gospel. The sacraments are literally an embodiment and demonstration of the gospel.

Baptism and the Eucharist (Holy Communion) are integral parts of our stewardship responsibility. And let's not forget prayer. This is the time where we talk with God and God talks with us. This is where God reveals his will, desires, vision, hopes, and dreams for his church and the world.

I would like to backtrack for a moment. Let's talk some more about the ministries of your congregation. The reason I want to do this is simply because I believe it is one of the places where many congregations make their biggest mistakes and fail to take advantage of one of their greatest opportunities. They talk about bucks and budgets instead of ministries. They talk about dollars and cents instead of their mission.

Let me just give you one example.

Worship Ministry

Organist Salary	$1,200.00
Choir Music	$ 300.00
Candles	$ 625.00
Communion Supplies	$ 475.00
Bulletins and Inserts	$1,800.00
Supply Pastor	$ 325.00
Total	$4,725.00

Believe it or not, this is how the worship ministry of the congregation is often presented. When members look at this all they can see are dollar signs and numbers. Is this an honest picture of your congregation's worship ministry?

Instead, shouldn't this be where the gospel, which has the power to save, to convert, and to change people's lives, is proclaimed? Isn't this the place where you not only hear but also receive the entire forgiveness of all your sins? Isn't this where the Holy Spirit gives you guidance and strength for daily living? Isn't this where the Lord empowers and equips you for ministry?

Why doesn't your congregation get rid of the numbers and dollar signs and put a ministry narrative in its place that describes the marvelous ways God is present in the midst of your church, touching people's lives with his grace, love, and power? Do you see the significant difference between the two forms?

Do you see why we have so much trouble raising our church's budget? Is it any wonder people don't want to pledge to the budget? We shouldn't even have budgets. Instead, we should have investments in mission or a ministry spending plan. This should only happen after people have committed themselves, their time, and their possessions to the ministries and the mission of Christ's church. We need to teach people to give in grateful response to God and out of love and commitment to Jesus Christ and his church and mission.

Let's talk for a few moments about other ways most congregations encourage and nurture a bucks and budgets or dollars and cents kind of perception in the life of their members. It is called financial statements. These come in two forms.

Financial Statement #1

Our records indicate that you pledged $_____. To date, you have given $_____.

Financial Statement #2

Date	Amount Given		
1/3	$5.00		
1/10	$5.00		
1/17	$5.00		
1/24	$5.00		
2/14	$10.00		
2/21	$5.00		
3/8	$5.00		
3/15	$5.00		
3/29	$5.00		
		Total amount given	$50.00

And again, all we have done is to reinforce the old dollars and cents perception of the church.

How would you feel if you opened an envelope from your church and found this instead:

Dear Frank and Marie,

Thank you for the offerings and gifts of $50.00 you have given these past three months. Your offerings and those of the other members of our congregation totaled $72,345!

Just look at the ministries those gifts and offerings have made possible here at Servant of Christ Lutheran Church.

Each Sunday morning, an average of ninety-seven children, youth, and adults gather to study God's Word. That has given the Holy Spirit the opportunity to work directly in each one of these people's lives, giving new insights, strengthening faith, and helping to prepare them for ministry in their daily life.

Part of our offerings is shared with the synod, the ELCA, and worldwide for ministries and missions like these:

> One hundred twenty-three new missions are under development. Five of them are right here in our own synod. Between 40 percent and 80 percent of the persons being received into these new missions are people who, until now, have been unchurched. Isn't that exciting?

Thank you for your offerings and gifts and for the very significant ministries and missions you are making possible.

Your Partner in Ministry,

Grace Givings, Financial Secretary

*For income tax purposes, a detailed record of your offerings is attached to this letter.

Do you see the significant difference between the two approaches? Just a little switch like this can change people's perception from bucks and budgets to ministries and mission. Don't you think it is worth the effort? You bet it is!

While we're on the subject of giving and gifts, please accompany me on an intellectual safari into some of the gifts that are given to Christ's church. I would like to preface this by saying that where God and giving are concerned, God always "Hallmarks"—he always cares enough to send the very best. Jesus Christ is, of course, the supreme example of that.

When it comes to our giving, why don't we Hallmark ss God does, instead of following practices like these. Come on folks. Let's put some real Hallmark into our giving to Christ and his Church, instead of falling into practices like this:

1. I can't use this anymore, Pastor, and I was wondering if the church would like to have it?
2. Let's get it as cheap as we can.
3. I'm going to get a new one and wondered if the church would like this old one?
4. Let's see. I have to buy this, that, and the other thing. Whatever is left can go into the offering.
5. Once we know the date and time of the Super Bowl, we can schedule the annual meeting.

Chapter 4

Giving

You knew, when we started this venture, that sooner or later we would be talking about giving. You may be surprised that this topic didn't come much sooner.

Notice, please, that the topic here is "Giving" and not "Money."

While money is, indeed, a part of what is included when we talk about giving, it is ONLY that =ONE part of what is involved in giving.

There is a point in the worship service when the offerings of the people and the bread and the wine used in Holy Communion are brought to the altar. This is when the congregation prays one of the most powerful, little prayers I know from *The Lutheran Book of Worship*. It says, "Heavenly Father, we offer with joy and thanksgiving what you have first given us, ourselves, our time, and our possessions, signs of Your gracious love."

Pause long enough to read this prayer again. Isn't it powerful? This prayer says it all. When we give, we should give all that we have and are. Please understand how much fun, excitement, and happiness this can bring you. I know this is contrary to everything you've ever heard or ever been taught about giving. Hang on friend. You're about to be introduced to a whole new way of thinking, and I think you're going to like it!

I will remind you that everything we have and everything we are is very graciously entrusted to us by the God who is its Creator and Lord. As you recall, that means that everything we have and are is a trust from God. We are the managers, the trustees, the caretakers, and the administrators of it all. We must do this according to God's will, desires, hopes, design, and own practice and example.

When we look at the way God does things, we see that everything is saturated with giving. God gives us life and breath. God gives us everything we need to sustain our lives.

I made a mistake here. I had God acting like us, instead of the other way around!

God doesn't just give life and breath to us. God gives it to all creatures and all people. Don't just take my word for it. Listen to what Jesus has to say on that score, "He [your heavenly Father] makes his sun rise on the evil and on the good, and sends rain on the just and on the unjust" (Matt. 5:45). These words come right out of what we call the Sermon on the Mount. In this sermon, Jesus points out how God cares for the birds and clothes the fields. Jesus then goes on to emphasize that if God so completely cares for and supplies the needs of the birds, beasts, and fields, he will certainly care much more for humans, who are God's children.

Again, this is all about giving. What God gives us is not something we earn or merit. It is something that God freely gives to us. God is not required to give it to us but chooses to.

Now we have come to the Holy of Holies in giving. John 3:16–17 will tell us what it is, "God so loved the world that he gave his only Son, that whoever believes in him should not perish but have eternal life. For God sent the Son into the world, not to condemn the world, but that the world might be saved through him." It says in 1 John 1:9–10, "In this the love of God was made manifest among us, that God sent [gave] his only Son into the world, so that we might live through him. In this is love, not that we loved God but that he loved us and sent [gave] his Son to be the expiation for our sins." This is astounding! It is even more so when we remember this took place while we were yet sinners.

Once again, remember, as God's stewards (entrusted ones) we are to manage, care for, use, and administer all that God has given us in the same way God would. We must act, work, and behave the way he does. First and foremost, this takes the form of giving. As we give, we are being godlike.

I'll tell you something else. God knew what he was doing when he commanded, encouraged, and reminded us to give. Look at the Dead Sea. What does the Dead Sea have to do with God commanding us to give? Everything! Let me explain.

What is it that makes the Dead Sea dead? It receives water from several different sources but has no outlets. It takes what it gets and holds onto it. Consequently, it stagnates. Because there is no outflow, no oxygen is generated. Thus, the Dead Sea cannot support any form of life.

Do you see my point? Giving is not only healthy but also essential for life. Unless we give, we become selfish, greedy, and hoarding. These characteristics squeeze the life right out of us.

Selfish, greedy, and grasping people are dying (or already dead) people. That's why they're so miserable, cranky, cold, impersonal, and desperate. Besides this, in every sense of the biblical word, they are idolaters.

Think of the people you know who are truly happy and whose lives are full and rich—people who are really alive. Who are they? They are the folks who give themselves away and who are living for others. They are the ones whose time and possessions are being invested in, used for, and given to other people. They are meeting other people's needs and are making other people's lives richer and fuller.

It is my firm conviction that God loves to see a cheerful giver. He knows that person has found the secret to the rich, full, and happy life God has for him.

Please allow me to share my own personal convictions, beliefs, and philosophy about giving. I believe God gives us to one another as a gift. People are among the richest gifts God gives us. Like all of God's gifts, we are to receive other people with thanksgiving. The diversity of these people makes for richness. We should respect and accept all people. We have the opportunity to be godlike when we give ourselves, our time, and our possessions so that others can have life, health, joy, and Jesus Christ.

Chapter 5

What Giving Means To Me

Giving Is Opportunity

1. Giving is the opportunity to express my gratitude to God.

God has blessed me! God has filled my life with his goodness, mercies, and grace. He has not just filled my life but has caused it to overflow way beyond what I need, have any right to expect, and my wildest dreams.

Let's read what the apostle Paul wrote to the Christians in Corinth. As you read, see if this describes your life and your experience. "And God is able to provide you with every blessing in abundance, so that you may always have enough of everything and may provide in abundance for every good work ... You will be enriched in every way for great generosity, which through us will produce thanksgiving to God" (2 Cor. 9:8, 11).

Is this an accurate description of your life? God has blessed, is blessing, and will bless us in this way.

So far we've only mentioned physical and material blessings, mercies, and goodness, which God has poured into our lives. We haven't even mentioned the greatest of all blessings—God's Son, Jesus Christ, and his forgiveness, life, deliverance, hope, and glory, which is ours.

Let's review. Giving is having the opportunity to express my gratitude to God through my offering.

2. Giving is the opportunity to acknowledge the Lordship of God.

Again and again, it is the affirmation of Holy Scripture that "the earth is the Lord's and the fulness thereof" (Ps. 24:1). All I am and have belongs to God.

God is the Creator, the giver, the true and rightful owner, and the Lord of all. All that I am and all I have is a trust from God. It is granted to me for management, care, and use, but it all belongs to God. All that I am belongs to God.

When I give of my time, possessions, and myself, it is an expression of who these things really belong to and a real opportunity to acknowledge God's lordship in my life.

My giving—proportionate giving, giving of firstfruits, and off-the-top giving—provides the opportunity to truly acknowledge that God is, indeed, the Lord of everything.

3. Giving is the opportunity to be a worker together with God.

Let's review what Saint Paul says as he addresses the Christians in Corinth, "If any one is in Christ, he is a new creation; the old has passed away, behold, the new has come. All this is from God, who through Christ reconciled us to himself and gave us the ministry of reconciliation … So we are ambassadors for Christ, God making his appeal through us" (2 Cor. 5:17–20).

Do you see how exciting life can be? You could be asking for so much more meaning and purpose in your life.

God's whole eternal purpose is expressed in the Great Commission we have received from our Lord Jesus Christ, "Go therefore and make disciples of all nations, baptizing them in the name of the Father and of the Son and of the Holy Spirit, teaching them to observe all that I have commanded you; and lo, I am with you always, to the close of the age" (Matt. 28:19–20).

Isn't this marvelous? God has this terribly important work that must be accomplished and deliberately chooses us to work with him in bringing it to pass. When we give, the presence, love, caring, and blessing of God can be known and experienced by other people.

Don't forget our daily bread. Remember how our Lord fed the five thousand when they needed it? Jesus took the bread and the fish the disciples had brought to him. He blessed it, broke it, and then put it into the disciple's hands to distribute. Everyone was fed.

4. Giving is the opportunity to join other believers and stewards to do together what none of us could do by ourselves.

This is why the ministries and the mission of our congregations, synods, and the whole church worldwide are so terribly important. Your offerings are what make them possible, strong, and effective.

Let me try to give you an idea of how desperately the church's ministries are needed and why your generous giving is so vital to these ministries. As I write this book, my denomination—The Evangelical Lutheran Church in America—has 123 new ministries under development all across the United States. It has five hundred missionaries in forty-nine countries who are doing a variety of ministries. A local Lutheran social service agency has recently completed its four thousandth adoption! These are ministries that we can only do together and none of us can do alone.

5. Giving is the opportunity to test the sincerity of my faith, the genuineness of my love, and the level of my commitment.

It is easy for me to say, "I believe," "Jesus Christ is my Lord," and "I love you, God." But the way I give tests and demonstrates whether what I say is true or is just a bunch of empty words.

Think about some of our bumper stickers. A popular one says, "Honk if you love Jesus." This sticker doesn't cost us anything and makes no demands of us. Honking and waving is no real test of how sincere our faith is, how genuine our love is, or how deep our commitment is. My neighbor has a bumper sticker that is much more to the point. It reads, "TITHE if you love Jesus, anybody can honk!"

Whether I give, how much I give, and the spirit in which I give are a demonstration and an evidence of the sincerity of my faith, the genuineness of my love, and the depth of my commitment. The Lord Jesus Christ, who redeemed us and made us his own by suffering death on the cross, has demonstrated the genuineness of his love for me.

When I give and it costs me something, it provides an opportunity to show the genuineness of my love for Jesus Christ and for his church and mission.

6. Giving is an opportunity to grow.

When I was a boy, my mother used to give me a dollar to put in the offering each week until the day I received my first paycheck.

She said, "No more, George. Now you are going to have to use your own money and make your own decision as to what you are going to give as an offering."

Each year, my congregation sets before me the same need for decision. I consider God's blessings, his lordship over my life, my possessions, and the demands and opportunities there are for ministries and mission. I also consider the possibilities of giving more and of boldly responding to the gracious calling of my Lord and God.

Printed in the United States
By Bookmasters